THE FUTURE
OF EDUCATION .

A PIONEERING
CASE STUDY

PETER CHEW

PCET VENTURES (003368687-P)

Email:peterchew999@hotmail.my

© Peter Chew 2023

Cover Design : Peter Chew

Cover Image: Freepik Premium

Mathematician, Inventor and Biochemist Peter Chew

Peter Chew is Mathematician, Inventor and Biochemist. Global issue analyst, Reviewer for Europe Publisher, Engineering Mathematics Lecturer and President of Research and Development Secondary School (IND) for Kedah State Association [2015-18].

Peter Chew received the Certificate of appreciation from Malaysian Health Minister Datuk Seri Dr. Adam Baba(2021), PSB Singapore. National QC Convention STAR AWARD (2 STAR), 2019 Outstanding Analyst Award from IMRF (International Multidisciplinary Research Foundation), IMFR Inventor Award 2020 , the Best Presentation Award at the 8th

International Conference on Engineering Mathematics and Physics ICEMP 2019 in Ningbo, China , Excellent award (Silver) of the virtual International, Invention, Innovation & Design Competition 2020 (3iDC2020) and Jury in the International Teaching and Learning Invention, Innovation Competition (iTaLiiC2023).

Analytical articles published in local and international media. Author for more than 60 Books , 8 preprint articles published in the World Health Organization (WHO) and 36 article published in the Europe PMC.

Peter Chew also is CEO PCET, Ventures, Malaysia, PCET is a long research associate of IMRF (International Multidisciplinary Research Foundation), Institute of higher Education & Research with its HQ at India and Academic Chapters all over the world, PCET also Conference Partner in CoSMEd2021 by SEAMEO RECSAM.

Peter Chew as 2nd Plenary Speaker the 6th International Multidisciplinary Research Conference with a Mindanao Zonal Assembly on January 14, 2023, at the Immaculate Conception University, Bajada Campus, Davao City.

Keynote Speaker of the 8th International Conference on Computer Engineering and Mathematical Sciences (ICCEMS 2019) , the International Conference on Applications of Physics , Chemistry & Engineering Sciences, ICPCE 2020 , 2nd Global Summit on Public Health and Preventive Medicine (GSPHPM2023) June 19, 2023 and World BIOPOLYMERS & POLYMER CHEMISTRY CONGRESS" 10-11 July 2023 | Online by Drug Delivery,

Special Talk Speaker at the 2019 International Conference on Advances in Mathematics, Statistics and Computer Science, the 100th CONF of the IMRF,2019, Goa , India.

Invite Speaker of the 24th Asian Mathematical Technology Conference (ATCM 2019) Leshan China , the 5^{th}(2020), 6th (2021) and 7th (2022) International Conference on Management, Engineering, Science, Social Sciences and Humanities by Society For Research Development(SRD) and 12th International Conference on Engineering Mathematics and Physics (July 5-7, 2023 in Kuala Lumpur, Malaysia).

Peter Chew is also Program Chair for the 11th International Conference on Engineering Mathematics and Physics (ICEMP 2022, Saint-Étienne, France | July 7-9, 2022) and Program Chair for the 12th International Conference on Engineering Mathematics and Physics (ICEMP 2023, Kuala Lumpur, Malaysia | July 5-7, 2023).

For more information, please get it from this link Orcid: https://orcid.org/0000-0002-5935-3041.

THE FUTURE OF EDUCATION
A PIONEERING CASE STUDY

TABLE OF CONTENTS

THE FUTURE OF EDUCATION
A PIONEERING CASE STUDY

TABLE OF CONTENTS

The Future of Education . A Pioneering Case Study

Introduction:

This book presents a case study conducted at Phor Tay Secondary School, Penang, Malaysia, focused on the implementation of the Education 4.0 Calculator Learning Method. This study explore how this innovative approach is reshaping education for the future, offering valuable insights, challenges, and successes during its implementation. A Education 4.0 Calculator Learning Method workshop was held to assess the effectiveness of the Education 4.0 Calculator Learning Method in secondary education.

Method:

The workshop was structured into two distinct parts. The first segment introduced fundamental concepts, including Peter Chew's Rule, Method, and triangle diagrams.

The second segment cantered on the Education 4.0 Calculator Learning Method, which was complemented by the utilization of advanced tools like Mathportal , Wolfram Alpha and Symbolab to provide a comparative perspective.

Results:

The implementation of the Education 4.0 Calculator Learning Method during the workshop proved to be highly successful. Significantly, five out of six participating teachers admitted to having no prior knowledge of Peter Chew's Rule, Method, and Triangle Diagram prior to the workshop.

This lack of knowledge had previously hindered their ability to efficiently solve all triangle-related problems simple, just need to use one rule and only once. However, following the workshop, all participants expressed increased confidence in their ability to solve all triangle-related problems simple, just need to use one rule and only once.

One teacher did have prior knowledge of Peter Chew's Rule, Method, and Triangle Diagram, enabling her to solve all triangle-related problems simple, just need to use one rule and only once even before the workshop.

All six teachers unanimously endorsed the integration of Peter Chew's Triangle Diagram and the Education 4.0 Calculator Learning Method into the Malaysian Ministry of Education's Additional Mathematics curriculum.

This integration is expected to enhance the teaching and learning of Solution of Triangle Topics (KSSM, Level 4), ultimately leading to more effective educational outcomes.

Conclusion:

This study highlights the transformative impact of the Education 4.0 Calculator Learning Method at Phor Tay Secondary School. Moreover, all six teachers found Peter Chew's Method and Rule to be more accessible and effective compared to conventional approaches when solving triangle-related problems.

The Educational 4.0 Calculator was recognized as a user-friendly tool that significantly enhances the teaching and learning of Solution of Triangle Topics (KSSM, Level 4). These findings underscore the potential for innovative educational methods and tools to revolutionize the teaching and learning experience.

Keyword: Education 4.0 Calculator Learning Method, Phor Tay Secondary School.

1. Introduction:

Industry 4.0 [1] requires employees who are critical thinkers, innovators, digitally skilled and problem solvers. The problem in the future is not the lack of jobs, but the lack of skills that new jobs will demand.

Therefore, the Objective of the Education Calculator Learning Method 4.0 is to develop the skills required by the Industry 4.0 labor market, such as problem-solving and digital skills.

The 21st century has witnessed a rapid transformation in the field of education, driven by the relentless advance of digital technologies and the need for innovative teaching methodologies.

This study delves into the intricacies of the Education 4.0 Calculator Learning Method and its role in shaping secondary education. Education has entered an era where technology, once perceived as an aid to the learning process, has become an integral part of the pedagogical landscape.

This paradigm shift, often referred to as Education 4.0, marks a transition from traditional, teacher-centered instruction to more interactive, learner-centric methodologies. The process of integrating these transformative methods into the classroom setting and their effectiveness in enhancing the educational experience remains a critical topic of discussion and exploration.

Penang Education Department supports the recommendation of Education Calculator 4.0 to SPM (Sijil Pelajaran Malaysia) students and STPM (Sijil Tingi Persekolahan Malaysia) students.

From previous study, "The Education 4.0 Calculator Learning Method workshop[2], conducted at the Center Prai and Chio Min Secondary School, has demonstrated remarkable success. Upon attending the Education 4.0 Calculator Workshop, all 25 teachers from Center Prai unanimously confirmed their mastery of the Education 4.0 Calculator for solving intricate triangle problems methodically, following a single rule, and doing so with a single iteration.

Feedback from the SISC+ Science and Mathematics Officer of the Seberang Prai Tengah District Education Office, Penang, Tuan Ong Khye Ching.

I am excited by Dr Peter Chew's sharing of Rules, Methods and Peter Chew Triangle Diagrams and Educational 4.0 Calculator. This workshop adds new knowledge and skills in teaching the topic of solving triangles. Using Peter Chew Rule, Methods and Triangle Diagrams can solve triangle problems with simple solutions.

Education 4.0 Calculator introduced by Dr Peter Chew is a new teaching and learning application that can help improve the quality and effectiveness of student learning in the topic of solution of triangles (KSSM Supplementary Mathematics Form 4). I hope that this new knowledge and skills can be disseminated to Additional Mathematics teachers throughout Malaysia.

I suggest that Peter Chew's Rule, Methods and Triangle Diagrams can be published in the Additional Mathematics curriculum to provide more alternative options for students in solving triangle problem.

Equally significant is the response from the 24 students of Chio Min Secondary School who participated in the Educational Calculator Workshop 4.0. They too have acquired the proficiency to employ the Educational Calculator 4.0 with precision, comprehensively addressing triangle problems step-by-step, adhering to a single rule, and achieving optimal results with a single application.

Feedback from Additional Mathematics Teacher SMJK Chio Min, Kulim, Kedah, Teacher Phong Bee Bee.

Educational 4.0 Calculator is easy to use, easy to install and easy to access offline. Educational 4.0 Calculator is easy to use to find the final answer to triangle problems because it is user friendly.Educational 4.0 Calculator helps solve triangle problems step by step with a single tip because the steps are clear and systematic.

The Education 4.0 calculator learning method is more interesting than the current learning method. I recommend Malaysia to use the Education 4.0 calculator learning method compared to the current learning method because the Education 4.0 calculator learning method is easy to understand, very suitable for students and easy to use.

This unequivocal success underscores the effectiveness of the Education 4.0 Calculator Learning Method in equipping both educators and students with a powerful tool for enhancing their mathematical skills and problem-solving capabilities."

Notably, in Malaysia, the Ministry of Education has been actively pursuing reforms in the education sector, recognizing the need to prepare students for a world characterized by rapid technological advancements and the evolving demands of the job market.

In this regard, innovative educational methods and tools, such as the Education 4.0 Calculator Learning Method, have become the subject of significant interest and debate. This study, conducted in collaboration with Phor Tay Secondary School, contributes to the ongoing dialogue surrounding the integration of such methods into mainstream education.

1.1 Simple Knowledge

Simple knowledge is the most important core of Education 4.0. Simple knowledge will make teaching and learning more effective and enjoyable. Simple knowledge can help self learning, Learn anytime, anywhere. Knowledge can be learned outside the classroom.

Simple solutions can improve the efficiency of teaching and learning, prevent math phobia, reduce errors, and provide accurate answers in many case and enhancing problem-solving skills, developing a problem-solving mindset, develop critical thinking and analytical skills required for Industry 4.0.

In Addition, Simple solutions can definitely enhance problem-solving learning methods , enhance experiential learning methods, ultimately lead to better math results, a crucial component of Education 4.0 and essential for online calculators and AI apps development.

1.1.1) Simple rules and solutions can improve the efficiency of teaching and learning

Using simple math methods can improve teaching and learning efficiency. For one, simpler methods can help students understand math concepts more easily, which can lead to greater confidence and engagement with the subject.

Additionally, simpler methods can reduce the cognitive load on students, allowing them to focus more on the underlying concepts and less on the mechanics of solving problems.

Finally, simpler methods can be more efficient to teach, as they may require less time to explain and result in fewer errors and misconceptions.

Overall, using simple math methods can be a great way to improve efficiency and effectiveness in math education.

1.1.2 Simple math solutions ultimately lead to better math results.

Using more simple math solutions not only helps save time for teaching and learning the material, but it also frees up time for students to study other chapters, revise and reinforcement of knowledge can help students better understand the material and ultimately lead to better math results.

Answering some exam questions using simple math solutions can help students save time, boost their confidence and reduce stress during exams, freeing up more time to answer additional questions. This can ultimately lead to better math results

1.1.3) Simple rules and solutions can prevent math phobia

Simple solution can breaking down problems into simple steps and using basic math methods, people are better able to understand and approach mathematics. This can help build their confidence and reduce feelings of anxiety or fear related to math.

Furthermore, using simple math methods can also help individuals see the practical applications of math in everyday life. This can help demystify math and make it more relatable and less abstract. By seeing how math is used in real-world situations, people can begin to appreciate its importance and relevance, which can further reduce math phobia

Many student suffer from math phobia, which is a fear or anxiety related to math. One reason why simple math methods can help alleviate math phobia is that they provide an easy and accessible way for individuals to learn and understand mathematical concepts.

Often, math phobia arises when individuals feel overwhelmed or intimidated by complex mathematical problems.

1.1.4) Simple rules and solutions can reduce errors.

Simple solution provide less room for error: The more complex a mathematical method is, the easier it is to make mistakes or overlook important details. Simple methods, on the other hand, are often straightforward and leave little room for misinterpretation.

1.1.5) Simple rules and solutions provide more accurate answers in many case.

Using simple math solutions with fewer intermediate approximations can help reduce the potential for errors to accumulate and result in a less accurate final answer. This is because each intermediate approximation introduces a certain amount of error or uncertainty, and these errors can propagate through subsequent calculations, leading to larger and larger deviations from the true solution.

Therefore, by minimizing the number of intermediate approximations, simple math solutions can lead to a more accurate final answer in many case.

1.1.6) Simple math solutions enhancing problem-solving skills , developing a problem-solving mindset, develop critical thinking and analytical skills required for Industry 4.0.

Simple math solutions can enhance problem-solving skills because they provide a structured and logical approach to problem-solving.

Math involves breaking down complex problems into smaller, more manageable pieces, which is a key skill in problem-solving.

Additionally, practicing simple math solutions can help individuals develop critical thinking and analytical skills, which are essential for effective problem-solving. It can also improve one's ability to recognize patterns, identify trends, and make informed decisions.

Furthermore, simple math solutions can help individuals develop a problem-solving mindset that can be applied to a wide range of situations, not just mathematical problems.

The skills and techniques used in math problem-solving, such as reasoning, logical deduction, and creative thinking, can be transferred to other areas of problem-solving.

Overall, simple math solutions can be a valuable tool for enhancing problem-solving skills , developing a problem-solving mindset, develop critical thinking and analytical skills that can help individuals tackle a wide range of challenges in their personal and professional lives.

1.1.7 Using simple math solutions can definitely enhance problem-solving learning methods. When the solution to a problem is complex, it can be very difficult for students to solve it on their own.

As a result, teachers may resort to traditional teaching methods where they simply lecture to the students. However, this approach is not effective in developing problem-solving skills that are necessary for industry 4.0. Using simple math solutions can help students better understand the problem-solving process and develop their own problem-solving skills. This approach allows teachers to focus more on guiding students through the process instead of just presenting a complex solution.

By doing so, students also can develop critical thinking and analytical skills that are essential for success in the current Industry 4.0 era. These skills are highly valued by employers who seek candidates with the ability to think creatively and solve complex problems in the workplace.

1.1.8 Simple math solutions can definitely enhance experiential learning methods or "learn by doing" methods.

When solutions are complex, students may struggle to solve problems on their own, which can lead to a reliance on traditional teaching methods where the teacher simply lectures to the students.

However, this can be less effective in helping students learn. By using simple math solutions, students can better understand the problem-solving process and actively participate in the learning experience. This approach allows them to develop their own problem-solving skills and apply them to real-world situations

Experiential learning methods are very effective because they allow students to actively engage with the material, which helps them remember it better and apply it in various contexts. As Benjamin Franklin once said, "Tell me and I forget, teach me and I may remember, involve me and I learn."

1.1.9 Simple knowledge is a crucial component of Education 4.0.

When knowledge is presented in a simple and accessible way, it can make teaching and learning more effective and enjoyable. Simple knowledge can help students learn on their own, at their own pace and in their own space, which can be very beneficial in today's fast-paced and ever-changing world.

By making knowledge simple and accessible, students can learn anytime, anywhere, and outside of the traditional classroom setting. This approach can help students become more self-directed learners, which is essential for success in the modern era.

With simple knowledge, students can easily access materials and resources, which can help them deepen their understanding and develop new skills.

1.1.10 Simple knowledge essential for online calculators and AI apps development.

Simple knowledge can be easily programmed into educational technology tools such as online calculators and AI apps. This can encourage the development of more educational technology tools that are inclusive of technology and can help make teaching and learning more relevant in Education 4.0. With these tools, students can learn more effectively and enjoyably.

These tools can help make the learning experience more engaging and interactive for students, and can also help teachers save time and focus on guiding students through the learning process.

Overall, the inclusion of simple knowledge in educational technology tools can help make teaching and learning more effective, fun, and relevant in Education 4.0.

1.1.11 Albert Einstein's quote

i) We cannot solve our problems with the same thinking we used when we created them .

ii)Everything should be made as simple as possible, but not simpler.

iii) If you can't explain it simply you don't understand it well enough

iv) Genius is making complex ideas simple, not making simple ideas complex.

v). "Any intelligent fool can make things bigger and more complex. It takes a touch of genius - and a lot of courage - to move in the opposite direction."

vi) God always takes the simplest way.

vii) When the solution is simple, God is answering.

Isaac Newton quote Nature is pleased with simplicity. And nature is no dummy.

From the Albert Einstein's and *Isaac Newton* quote above,

it can be seen that simplifying knowledge is very important.

2 new simple solutions available on the Education 4.0 calculator,

i) Peter Chew Method [3] for solving triangles can solve the same triangle problem very easily compared to the current method.

ii). Peter Chew Rule [4] for solving triangles can solve same triangle problems easily and more accurately than current methods.

With these two new simple knowledge, the Education 4.0 calculator, Peter Chew Triangle Diagram Calculator can guide users to solve all triangle problems with simple solutions, only need to use one Rule and only Once.

1.2 Problem-Based Learning Innovation

Using Problems to Power Learning in the 21st Century by Oon-Seng Tan PhD Associate Professor and Head of Psychological Studies National Institute of Education Nanyang Technological University Singapore .[5] Problem-based learning,[6] provides a unique and intriguing mechanism to move higher education beyond its traditional foundations and create the kinds of critical thinkers the labour market demands.

Most of the current literature on the "future of work" underscores the need for power skills, such as systems thinking, creativity, critical thinking, high emotional intelligence, communication, agility, resilience, and flexibility.

Employers are looking for candidates who can respond well in highly ambiguous situations and demonstrate a strong grasp of initiative, resolve and ethical judgment. And yes, many are also looking for STEM skills.

Problem-based Learning (PBL) involves students being challenged to solve genuine problems from their discipline .[7] In addition to developing general skills such as critical thinking and abstract reasoning, PBL is an ideal way for students to apply their theoretical knowledge in an authentic way.

PBL is often used as a way for students to develop experience in the process of solving a problem, rather than simply seeking a 'correct' solution.

For this reason, problems used for PBL include well-defined ones with a clear solution (or set of possible solutions), as well as more loosely-defined ones or those without a known solution.

The Effectiveness of the Project-Based Learning (PBL) Approach as a Way to Engage Students in Learning .[8]

The prevalence of project-based learning (PBL) has increased significantly, contributing to serious discussions about its advent. PBL's critics doubt whether accentuating the practice supports teachers in using a technocratic method in education, instead of promoting instruction that is responsive to students' ideas.

Thus, this study aims to develop on using the effectiveness of the PBL approach, as a way to engage students in learning as well as to incorporate literature on the PBL method for educational purposes.

1.3 Experiential Learning.[9]

"Experiential [learning] is a philosophy and methodology in which educators purposefully engage with students in direct experience and focused reflection in order to increase knowledge, develop skills, and clarify values" (Association for Experiential Education, para. 2). Experiential learning is also referred to as learning through action, learning by doing, learning through experience, and learning through discovery and exploration, all which are clearly defined by these well-known maxims:

Tell me and I forget,

Teach me and I remember,

Involve me and I will learn.   ~ *Benjamin Franklin, 1750*

In their book, *Teaching for Experiential Learning,* Wurdinger and Carlson (2010) found that most college faculty teach by lecturing because few of them learned how to teach otherwise. Although good lecturing should be part of an educator's teaching repertoire, faculty should also actively involve their students "in the learning process through discussion, group work, hands-on participation, and applying information outside the classroom" (p. 2). This process defines experiential learning where students are involved in learning content in which they have a personal interest, need, or want.

1.3.1 WHAT IS EXPERIENTIAL LEARNING AND WHY IS IT IMPORTANT?[10]

Experiential Learning is the process of learning by doing. By engaging students in hands-on experiences and reflection, they are better able to connect theories and knowledge learned in the classroom to real-world situations.

Experiential learning opportunities exist in a variety of course- and non-course-based forms and may include community service, service-learning, undergraduate research, study abroad/away, and culminating experiences such as internships, student teaching, and capstone projects, to name a few.

When students participate in experiential education opportunities, they gain:

- A better understanding of course material

- A broader view of the world and an appreciation of community.

- Insight into their own skills, interests, passions, and values

- Opportunities to collaborate with diverse organizations and people.

- Positive professional practices and skill sets

- The gratification of assisting in meeting community needs

- Self-confidence and leadership skills.

1.3.2   Teaching critical 21st century skills through experiential learning.[11]

Experience : Concrete skills such as using computers or applications are often taught in a comprehensive, step-by-step manner, leaving little room for problem-solving and experimentation.   However,   problem-solving   and experimentation are fundamental to learning from experience. In this spirit, when assigning digital work, teachers should consider challenging students with the technology itself, just as they challenge the students with the assignment content or effort.

1.3.3 Using Technology for Experiential Learning.[12]

Simulation technologies. Common in a number of educational fields and are specifically designed to allow for "real-life" training and practice in a low risk environment.Flight simulation is a well-known example of this type of immersive technology that relies on sophisticated and expensive hardware and software. Health Science departments have adopted computer-enabled mannequins to provide an authentic experience in patient care and the application of knowledge.

1.4 Technology

1.4.1 The Future of Education: Integrating Technology in the Classroom.[13].

Integrating technology in the classroom requires expertise. To harness technology's power to make classrooms inclusive, interactive, and engaging, teachers need the right training.

Louisiana State University's <u>Master of Arts in Education with a concentration in Educational Technology</u> is designed to help teachers innovate ways to use technology and create exciting learning experiences.

How to Integrate Technology in the Classroom

Many learning technologies and tools boost a teacher's ability to engage students, as they facilitate access to a multitude of resources and interactive activities. Below are examples of technologies that can benefit teachers and students alike.

1.4.2 Integration of Technology in Teaching and Learning[14]

Comprehensive initiatives enhance student engagement and learning

As technology increasingly transforms our daily lives, educators too are seeking strategies and resources that leverage technology to improve student learning. Research demonstrates that high-quality professional development, digital standards based content, and personalized learning plans can increase student achievement, engagement, and critical-thinking skills, and provide students with access to learning opportunities otherwise difficult to attain.

What Is the National Policy Context Shaping the Integration of Technology into Teaching and Learning? The National Education Technology Plan 2010 (NETP) developed by the U.S. Department of Education Office of Educational Technology calls for a "revolutionary transformation" of our education system.

1.4.3 The Importance of Technological Integration in the Classroom.[15] *June 2022*

The COVID-19 pandemic necessitated the rapid implementation of technology into classrooms across America, but emerging technologies will remain a staple of learning environments even after the pandemic passes.

Today's children are simply too connected, and the potential benefits of tech integration in elementary education are too great for teachers to omit technology from their curricula. Instead, current and aspiring teachers should embrace technology as a tool that can accommodate various learning styles while also increasing student engagement.

Benefits

Finding the right balance is essential to realizing the full range of positive outcomes of integrating technology into your curriculum. According to Joe Marquez, a K-12 Education Strategist and certified Google Innovator, "it simply isn't wise to incorporate technology with bad instructional habits:

A screen should never take the place of a teacher or be used to babysit students." When technology is deployed within the framework of a carefully constructed lesson plan, however, it can lead to the following benefits:

- Improved student engagement
- Increased access for all students to learning opportunities
- Improved trust and stronger relationships between parents, teachers and students

1.4.4 Digital Transformation towards Education 4.0 .[16] 5 August 2022

The digital transformation of teaching processes is guided and supported by the use of technological, human, organizational and pedagogical drivers in a holistic way. Education 4.0 aims to equip students with cognitive, social, interpersonal, technical skills, among others, in the face of the needs of the Fourth Industrial Revolution and global challenges, such as mitigating the causes and effects of climate change based on people's awareness.

This work presents the development and experimentation of a method, called TADEO - acronym in Portuguese language to Transformação Digital na Educação (digital transformation in education), to guide the design and application of teaching and learning experiences from groups of drivers of the digital transformation in education, aiming to achieve Education 4.0 objectives.

The TADEO method was applied in the context of classes of basic subjects of elementary and higher education to increase students' understanding of climate change through the development of projects to mitigate environmental problems caused by anthropogenic action and, at the same time, exercise students the soft and hard skills required by 21st century learning and work.

The results of the evaluations of students and educators participating in the teaching and learning experiences guided by the TADEO method point to the achievement of the expected purposes.

1.4.5 Digital Revolution of Education 4.0.[17].

Beyond 21st century capabilities, abilities, advanced development, like Artificial Intelligence (AI), extensive information and research, distributed and portable computing systems, online networks, the Internet of Things (IoT), Virtual Reality (VR), Reality Augmented Computer Entertainment (AR) is transforming the educational process and progress into new computer-based learning methods, more generally smart-class products. The arrival of the Z generation with advanced information and digital capabilities has raised many challenges for teachers.

The current meaning of the Gen-Z consists of a dialect that is misunderstood by a more mature generation; you have your own type - a kind of computer. They have their own understanding and expression. Advanced locations use the powerful tools of the Internet and computer innovation to create imaginative, creative and expressive elements of digital security.

2. Method:

The workshop at Phor Tay Secondary School was meticulously planned and executed, featuring two distinct but complementary segments. The first segment served as a foundational introduction, acquainting participating secondary school teachers with fundamental mathematical concepts that included an exploration of Peter Chew's Rule, Method and Triangle Diagrams in triangle problem-solving. The second segment constituted the core of the workshop—the Education 4.0 Calculator Learning Method.

In the latter segment, participants were immersed in this innovative teaching approach, which is characterized by the seamless integration of digital tools into the learning process. The workshop also featured the utilization of advanced mathematical tools such as Mathportal Wolfram Alpha and Symbolab, which provided a comparative perspective on problem-solving techniques. This comprehensive approach aimed to elucidate the potential synergies between established mathematical principles and cutting-edge technology. In addition, **Feedback form have been set for evaluate the effectiveness of Peter Chew Rule, method, triangle diagram and Education 4.0 Calculator.**

2.1 The first segment served as a foundational introduction. acquainting participating secondary school teachers with fundamental mathematical concepts that included an exploration of Peter Chew's Rule, Method, and triangle diagrams in triangle problem-solving.

i) Peter Chew Method for Solution Of Triangle can solve the problem which is much easier, directly, than the current solution .

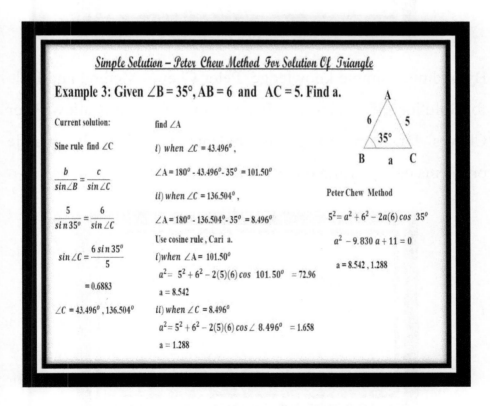

Simple Solution – Peter Chew Method For Solution Of Triangle

Example 3: Given $\angle B = 35°$, AB = 6 and AC = 5. Find a.

Current solution:

Sine rule find $\angle C$

$$\frac{b}{sin\angle B} = \frac{c}{sin\angle C}$$

$$\frac{5}{sin 35°} = \frac{6}{sin\angle C}$$

$$sin\angle C = \frac{6 sin 35°}{5}$$

$$= 0.6883$$

$\angle C = 43.496°, 136.504°$

find $\angle A$

i) when $\angle C = 43.496°$,

$\angle A = 180° - 43.496° - 35° = 101.50°$

ii) when $\angle C = 136.504°$,

$\angle A = 180° - 136.504° - 35° = 8.496°$

Use cosine rule , Cari a.

i)when $\angle A = 101.50°$

$a^2 = 5^2 + 6^2 - 2(5)(6) cos\ 101.50° = 72.96$

$a = 8.542$

ii) when $\angle C = 8.496°$

$a^2 = 5^2 + 6^2 - 2(5)(6) cos \angle 8.496° = 1.658$

$a = 1.288$

Peter Chew Method

$5^2 = a^2 + 6^2 - 2a(6) cos\ 35°$

$a^2 - 9.830\ a + 11 = 0$

$a = 8.542 , 1.288$

ii) Peter Chew Rule for Solution Of Triangle can solve the same problem simple, easily, more accurately than the current solution.

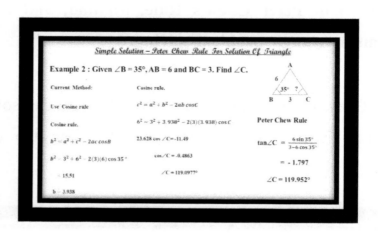

By adding 2 simple knowledge, Peter Chew's Method and Rule for Solution Of Triangle in Peter Chew's Diagrams allow Peter Chew's Diagrams to guide students to solve all triangle problems easily, using one Rule and only once.

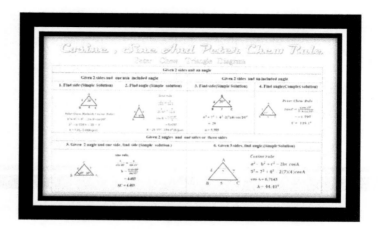

2.2 The second segment constituted the core of the workshop—the Education 4.0 Calculator Learning Method.

Advantage of **Education 4.0 Calculator compare others advanced tools like Mathportal**[18]**. , *Wolfram Alpha*[19]*. and Symbolab*[20]

2.2.1 Educational Calculator 4.0 guides student to use Peter Chew Triangle Diagrams for simple solution for all triangle problems. All problems can be solved easily with one Rule and only once.

This is most important for Educational Calculator Learning Method 4.0, because with simple solutions only teaching and learning can be more effective. Hence, Problem-based Learning, Experience-based Learning and self- Learning can be practice better.

If the solution is complex, of course self-learning is difficult to implement, because many student need to be teach individually . If the solution is complex, then the traditional teaching and learning method, through teacher teaching, may be more appropriate.

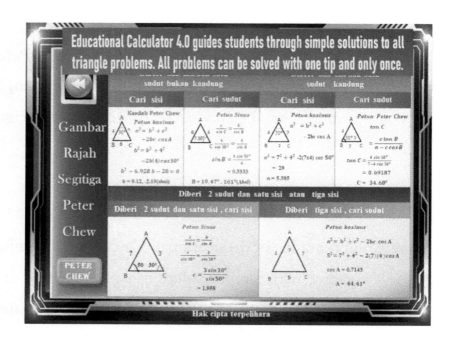

Other online calculators such as Mathportal guide user in using complex solution methods for some triangle problems.

Example 1: Complex solutions from Mathportal [Calculate on 9-12-2022].

problem	STEP 1: find angle γ	STEP 2: find angle α	STEP 3: find side a
Find side a of a triangle if side $b = 5$, side $c = 6$ and angle $\beta = 35°$	To find angle γ use The Law of Sines: $$\frac{\sin(\beta)}{b} = \frac{\sin(\gamma)}{c}$$ After substituting $b = 5$, $\beta = 35°$ and $c = 6$ we have: $$\frac{\sin(35°)}{5} = \frac{\sin(\gamma)}{6}$$ $$\frac{0.5736}{5} = \frac{\sin(\gamma)}{6}$$ $$\sin(\gamma) \cdot 5 = 0.5736 \cdot 6$$ $$\sin(\gamma) \cdot 5 = 3.4415$$ $$\sin(\gamma) = \frac{3.4415}{5}$$ $$\sin(\gamma) = 0.6883$$ $$\gamma = \arcsin 0.6883$$ $$\gamma \approx 43.495°$$	To find angle α use formula: $$\alpha + \beta + \gamma = 180°$$ After substituting $\beta = 35°$ and $\gamma = 43.495°$ we have: $$\alpha + 35° + 43.495° = 180°$$ $$\alpha + 78.495° = 180°$$ $$\alpha = 180° - 78.495°$$ $$\alpha = 101.505°$$	To find side a use Law of Cosines: $$a^2 = b^2 + c^2 - 2 \cdot b \cdot c \cdot \cos(\alpha)$$ After substituting $b = 5$, $c = 6$ and $\alpha = 101.505°$ we have: $$a^2 = 5^2 + 6^2 - 2 \cdot 5 \cdot 6 \cdot \cos(101.505°)$$ $$a^2 = 25 + 36 - 2 \cdot 5 \cdot 6 \cdot \cos(101.505°)$$ $$a^2 = 61 - 2 \cdot 30 \cdot \cos(101.505°)$$ $$a^2 = 61 - 60 \cdot (-0.1995)$$ $$a^2 = 61 - (-11.9672)$$ $$a^2 = 72.9672$$ $$a = \sqrt{72.9672}$$ $$a \approx 8.5421$$
solution $a \approx 8.5421$			

Example 2: Complex solutions from Mathportal [Calculate on 9-12-2022].

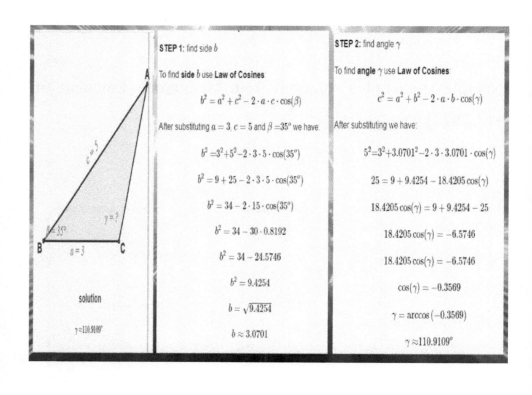

STEP 1: find side b

To find **side b** use **Law of Cosines**:

$$b^2 = a^2 + c^2 - 2 \cdot a \cdot c \cdot \cos(\beta)$$

After substituting $a = 3$, $c = 5$ and $\beta = 35°$ we have:

$$b^2 = 3^2 + 5^2 - 2 \cdot 3 \cdot 5 \cdot \cos(35°)$$

$$b^2 = 9 + 25 - 2 \cdot 3 \cdot 5 \cdot \cos(35°)$$

$$b^2 = 34 - 2 \cdot 15 \cdot \cos(35°)$$

$$b^2 = 34 - 30 \cdot 0.8192$$

$$b^2 = 34 - 24.5746$$

$$b^2 = 9.4254$$

$$b = \sqrt{9.4254}$$

$$b \approx 3.0701$$

STEP 2: find angle γ

To find **angle γ** use **Law of Cosines**:

$$c^2 = a^2 + b^2 - 2 \cdot a \cdot b \cdot \cos(\gamma)$$

After substituting we have:

$$5^2 = 3^2 + 3.0701^2 - 2 \cdot 3 \cdot 3.0701 \cdot \cos(\gamma)$$

$$25 = 9 + 9.4254 - 18.4205 \cos(\gamma)$$

$$18.4205 \cos(\gamma) = 9 + 9.4254 - 25$$

$$18.4205 \cos(\gamma) = -6.5746$$

$$18.4205 \cos(\gamma) = -6.5746$$

$$\cos(\gamma) = -0.3569$$

$$\gamma = \arccos(-0.3569)$$

$$\gamma \approx 110.9109°$$

solution

$\gamma \approx 110.9109°$

2.2.2 Education 4.0 Calculator provides complete and correct answers. This is also important for the Educational 4.0 Calculator Learning Method 4.0, because with a complete and correct solution only self-learning can be effective.If the solution is incomplete and incorrectly given by other online calculators such as Wolfram Alfa, Symbolab and Mathportal., of course self-learning is difficult to implement, because many questions will arise from students.

Therefore, the Educational Calculator 4.0 Learning Method if using other online calculators such as Wolfram Alfa, Symbolab and Mathportal, to replace the Educational 4.0 Calculator will be ineffective and may have the opposite effect.

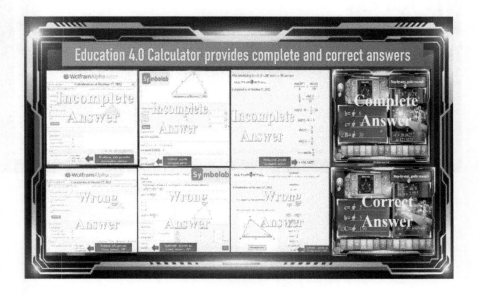

2.3 Education 4.0 Calculator vs Wolfram Alfa

	Education 4.0 Calculator	Wolfram Alfa
1. Cosine Rule	✓	✓
2. Sine Rule	✓	✓
3. Peter Chew Rule	✓	✗
4. Peter Chew Method	✓	✗
5. Peter Chew Triangle Diagram	✓	✗
6. Peter Chew Correction for Sine rule	✓	✗
Remarks	Correct , complete and simple solution and develop industry 4.0 skill	Some Incorrect , Incomplete and complex solution.

2.4 Feedback form have been set for evaluate the effectiveness of Peter Chew Rule, method, triangle diagram and Education 4.0 Calculator.

i) Feedback For The Solution Of Triangle Seminar.

Feedback For The Solution Of Triangle Seminar

Teacher's Name:_____ School:_____
Mobile Phone (Optional):_____ Email (optional): _____

1. Before the seminar, do you know Peter Chew Rule, Method and Triangle Diagrams? Yes □ , No □
Description (optional):
_____

2. Do you agree that Peter Chew's Method and Peter Chew's Rule are easier than the current method to solve the same triangle problem?   Yes □ , No □
Description (optional):
_____

3. Before the seminar, did you know how to solve all the triangle problems easily, just use one Rule and only once?   Yes □ , No □
Description (optional):
_____

4. After the seminar, do you know how to solve all the triangle problems easily, just use one Rule and only once?   Yes □ , No □
Description (optional):
_____

5. Do you agree that Peter Chew's Triangle Diagram makes teaching and learning Triangle Solution Topic (KSSM, Level 4) easier and more effective?   Yes □ , No □
Description (optional):
_____

6. Do you agree to introduce the Malaysian Ministry of Education to add Peter Chew's Triangle Diagram to the Additional Mathematics book to make the teaching and learning of Solution of Triangle Topics (KSSM, Level 4) more effective?   Yes □ , No □
Description (optional):
_____

Thank you for your feedback!

ii) Feedback Education 4.0 Calculator Workshop

Feedback Education 4.0 Calculator Workshop

Teacher's Name: _____   School: _____
Mobile Phone (Optional): _____   Email (optional): _____

1. Do you agree that Educational 4.0 Calculator is easy to use?   Yes □ , No □
Description (optional):
_____

2. After attending the Educational 4.0 Calculator Workshop, do you know how to use the Educational 4.0 Calculator to find the final answer to the triangle problem?
Yes □, No □
Description (optional):
_____

3. After attending the Educational 4.0 Calculator Workshop, You know how to use the Educational 4.0 Calculator to solve all triangle problems Step by Step with one Rule and only once. Yes □ , No □
Description (optional):
_____

4. Educational 4.0 Calculator has Malaysian and English versions, which version do you prefer?
                    Malay Version □ ,   English Version □
Description (optional):
_____

5. Do you agree that the Educational 4.0 Calculator learning method makes teaching and learning Solution of triangle Topics (KSSM, Level 4) more effective ? Yes □ , No □
Description (optional):
_____

6. Do you agree to introduce the Malaysian Ministry of Education to add the Education 4.0 calculator learning method to the current learning method to make teaching and learning more effective?
                    Yes □ , No □
Description (optional):
_____

Thank you for your feedback!

3. Results

The findings from the workshop shed light on the highly successful implementation of the Education 4.0 Calculator Learning Method. Particularly noteworthy is the fact that five out of the six participating teachers admitted to a prior lack of knowledge about Peter Chew's Rule, Method, and Triangle Diagram before attending the workshop.

This knowledge gap had previously posed significant obstacles to their ability to simple solve some triangle-related problems, which often necessitated the application of multiple rules and steps. However, following the workshop, teachers can simple solve these triangle problems . A single rule applied only once became the clarion call of efficiency.

Remarkably, one teacher stood out, possessing prior knowledge of Peter Chew's Rule, Method, and Triangle Diagram before workshop, enabling her to solve these triangle problems simple even before participating in the workshop.

Significantly, all six teachers unanimously rallied behind the idea of integrating Peter Chew's Triangle Diagram and the Education 4.0 Calculator Learning Method into the Malaysian Ministry of Education's Additional Mathematics curriculum.

This integration is anticipated to be a transformative force, destined to revolutionize the teaching and learning of Solution of Triangle Topics (KSSM, Level 4), with the ultimate goal of yielding more effective educational outcomes.

4. Discussion

The success of this workshop serves as a testament to the immense potential of innovative educational methods and tools to breathe new life into the teaching and learning experience within the realm of secondary education.

The Education 4.0 Calculator Learning Method, in particular, emerged as an effective strategy for simplifying complex mathematical problems, making them accessible to both students and teachers. By arming teachers with enhanced tools for instruction and students with a deeper understanding of mathematical concepts, this method has the power to elevate problem-solving skills and overall mathematical literacy.

The workshop's findings also highlighted the versatility of this approach. in addition, It holds promise in traditional classroom settings, the Education 4.0 Calculator Learning Method's also suitability for online and remote learning environments .

 In an era marked by the global shift towards virtual and blended learning, the adaptability and effectiveness of this method in various educational contexts hold significant relevance.

5. Conclusion

In conclusion, the workshop at Phor Tay Secondary School has effectively unveiled the transformative impact of the Education 4.0 Calculator Learning Method in a real-world educational setting. Beyond empowering teachers with accessible tools for instruction, the method has succeeded in enhancing teacher triangle problem-solving skills and providing a deeper comprehension of mathematical concepts.

Additionally, the Educational 4.0 Calculator has emerged as a user-friendly tool that significantly enriches the teaching and learning of Solution of Triangle Topics (KSSM, Level 4).

The unanimous endorsement of curriculum integration underscores the immense potential of these innovative educational methods and tools to bring about broader, positive transformations within the Malaysian education system.

By embracing the possibilities offered by Education 4.0 and digital tools, the education system is better equipped to prepare students for the challenges and opportunities that define the modern world.

6. Acknowledgement

6.1 Peter Chew Rule has passed peer review by The International Conference on Engineering Mathematics and Physics, ICEMP 2019. Peter Chew Rule collected in Journal of Physics: Conference Series (*J.Phys.: Conf. Ser.* 1411 012009

DOI 10.1088/1742-6596/1411/1/012009).Conference Proceedings Citation Index Scopus, Ei Compendex, etc.

Journal of Physics: Conference Series

PAPER • OPEN ACCESS

Peter Chew rule for solution of triangle

Peter Chew[1]

Published under licence by IOP Publishing Ltd

Journal of Physics: Conference Series, Volume 1411, 2019 the 8th International Conference on Engineering, Mathematics and Physics 1-3 July 2019, Ningbo, China

Citation Peter Chew 2019 J. Phys.: Conf. Ser. 1411 012009

DOI 10.1088/1742-6596/1411/1/012009

6.2 Best Presentation Award for Pete Chew Rule at the 8th International Conference on Engineering Mathematics and Physics ICEMP 2019 in Ningbo, China. http://www.icemp.org/history.html .

6.3 Invited speaker (Peter Chew Rule and PCET Calculator)of the 24th Asian Mathematics Technology Conference (ATCM 2019), Leshan China. https://atcm.mathandtech.org/EP2019/abstracts.html

6.4 Keynote Speaker (Peter Chew Rule and PCET Calculator) of the 8th International Conference on Computer Engineering and Mathematical Sciences (ICCEMS 2019.

https://www.iccems.com/2019/WB/v1/index.html@id=0.html

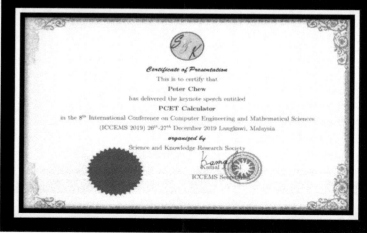

6.5 Keynote Speaker(Peter Chew Rule and PCET Calculator) the International Conference on Applications of Physics , Chemistry & Engineering Sciences, ICPCE 2020. , in <u>University Malaya, Malaysia.</u> <u>https://www.facebook.com/imrf.in/photos/a.354300178063577/14335071</u> <u>46809536/?type=3&theater</u> .

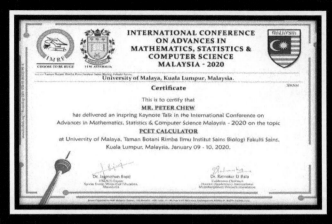

6.6 Special Talk Speaker at the 2019 International Conference on Advances in Mathematics, Statistics and Computer Science, the 100th CONF of the IMRF,2019, Goa , India, https://youtu.be/vviP5n02CEA

6.7 Peter Chew Rule and Peter Chew Method are simple solution in Peter Chew Triangle Diagram and Peter Chew Triangle Diagram has passed peer review by The 12th International Conference on Engineering Mathematics and Physics, ICEMP 2023.

6.8 Peter Chew Triangle Diagram(preprint) is share at World Health Organization because the purpose of Peter Chew Triangle Diagram is to help teaching mathematics more easily , especially when similar covid-19 problems arise in the future. https://pesquisa.bvsalud.org/global-literature-on-novel-coronavirus-2019-ncov/resource/en/ppzbmed-10.20944.preprints202106.0221.v1

6.9 Invited Speaker[Education 4.0 Calculator, Peter Chew Triangle Diagram Calculator] 7 th International Conference on Research Innovations (iCRI-22) Penang, Malaysia.11 Nov 2022. '7th **International Conference on Research Innovations' iCRI-2022 (Penang, Malaysia). Pautan iCRI-2022 [URL:** https://www.socrd.org/icri-22/] Minute to Minute Program of iCRI-22 [URL: https://www.socrd.org/wp-content/uploads/2022/10/MINUTE-TO-MINUTE-PROGRAM-iCRI-22.pdf .

6.10 Speaker for Workshop Education 4.0 Calculator , Peter Chew Triangle Diagram for 25 teacher from central Prai by District Education Office, Central Prai, Penang Malaysia.

6.11 2nd Plenary Speaker the 6th International Multidisciplinary Research Conference with a Mindanao Zonal Assembly on January 14, 2023, at the Immaculate Conception University, Bajada Campus, Davao *City*.

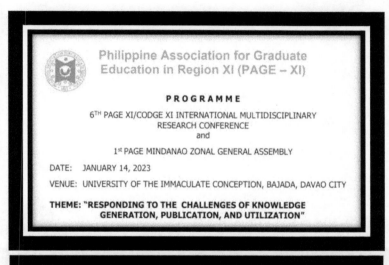

6.12 Invite Speaker on 12th International Conference on Engineering Mathematics and Physics (July 5-7, 2023) in Kuala Lumpur, Malaysia.

6.13 Best Presentation Award[Peter Chew Triangle Diagram] from International Conference on Engineering Mathematics and Physics (ICEMP 2023, July 5-7, 2023), KL, Malaysia .

7. **Reference**

1. INDUSTRY 4.0 AND ITS IMPACT ON EDUCATION. RESTART 4.0

https://restart-project.eu/industry-4-0-impact-education/

2. Chew, Peter, Education 4.0 Calculator Learning Method (December 20, 2022). Available at SSRN: https://ssrn.com/abstract=4307788 or http://dx.doi.org/10.2139/ssrn.4307788

3. Chew, Peter, Peter Chew Method For Solution Of Triangle (August 29, 2022). Available at SSRN:

https://ssrn.com/abstract=4203746 or http://dx.doi.org/10.2139/ssrn.4203746.

4. Peter Chew[1] · Peter Chew rule for solution of triangle. Published under licence by IOP Publishing Ltd Journal of Physics: Conference Series, Volume 1411, 2019 the 8th International Conference on Engineering, Mathematics and Physics 1–3 July 2019, Ningbo, China Peter Chew 2019 *J. Phys.: Conf. Ser.* 1411 012009 DOI 10.1088/1742-6596/1411/1/012009

5. Oon Seng Tan, Problem-Based Learning Innovation Using Problems to Power Learning in the 21st Century.

http://dspace.vnbrims.org:13000/jspui/bitstream/123456789/42
28/1/Problem-
based%20Learning%20Innovation%20Using%20problems%20
to%20power%20learning%20in%20the%2021st%20century.pd
f .

6. *Michelle R. Weise* Stop Talking and Start Doing: How to
Deliver 21st-Century Student Engagement and Education. The
evolllution, A modern Campus illumination.
https://evolllution.com/programming/teaching-and-
learning/stop-talking-and-start-doing-how-to-deliver-21st-
century-student-engagement-and-education/ Published on
2018/07/06 .

7. Ian Glover , Problem-based Learning: An Approach to
Teaching and Learning.
https://blogs.shu.ac.uk/shutel/2014/10/06/problem-based-
learning-an-approach-to-teaching-and-learning/ October 6,
2014

8. Mohammed Abdullatif Almulla , The Effectiveness of the
Project-Based Learning (PBL) Approach as a Way to Engage
Students in Learning. SAGE Journal
https://doi.org/10.1177/2158244020938702

9. Experiential learning .Northern Illinois University Center for Innovative Teaching and Learning. (2012). https://www.niu.edu/citl/resources/guides/instructional-guide/experiential-learning.shtml#:~:text=%E2%80%9CExperiential%20%5Blearning%5D%20is%20a,2)%20.

https://ruanofaxas.com/2012/03/10/paulina-rendon-aguilar-httpwww-linkedin-compubpaulina-rendon-aguilar3498b12-paulinarendona-2012-kennametal-global-marketing-summit-managers-effectiveness-award-kgms-kennametal/paulina-rendon-aguilar-kennametal-tell-me-and-i-forget-teach-me-and-i-may-remember-involve-me-and-i-learn/

10. Kent   WHAT IS EXPERIENTIAL LEARNING AND WHY IS IT IMPORTANT? KENT STATE UNIVERSITY. HTTPS://WWW.KENT.EDU/COMMUNITY/WHAT-EXPERIENTIAL-LEARNING-AND-WHY-IT-IMPORTANT

11. Teaching critical 21st century skills through experiential learning

LANSCHOOL   JANUARY   26,   2022. HTTPS://LANSCHOOL.COM/BLOG/EDUCATION-

INSIGHTS/TEACHING-CRITICAL-21ST-CENTURY-SKILLS-THROUGH-EXPERIENTIAL-LEARNING/

12. GWENNA MOSS CENTRE FOR TEACHING AND LEARNING, Using Technology for Experiential Learning. University of Saskatchewan . https://teaching.usask.ca/articles/using-technology-for-experiential-learning.php   Jan 23, 2017

13. The Future of Education: Integrating Technology in the Classroom.
LSU   Online   and   Continuing   Education. https://online.lsu.edu/newsroom/articles/future-education-integrating-technology-classroom/ March 25, 2020

14. Allison Nebbergall, Ph.D. et all Integration of Technology in   Teaching   and   Learning   . https://files.eric.ed.gov/fulltext/ED532587.pdf

15. The Importance of Technological Integration in the Classroom

University of Louisiana Monroc . Published On: June 15, 2022 https://online.ulm.edu/degrees/education/med/curriculum-and-instruction/technological-integration-in-the-classroom/

16. Katyeudo K. de S. OLIVEIRA1 , Ricardo A. C. de SOUZA. Digital Transformation towards Education 4.0 . Informatics in Education, 2022, Vol. 21, No. 2, 283–309 © 2022 Vilnius University, ETH Zürich DOI: 10.15388/infedu.2022.13

17. Priya Sharma, Digital Revolution of Education 4.0 . International Journal of Engineering and Advanced Technology (IJEAT) ISSN: 2249-8958 (Online), Volume-9 Issue-2, December, 2019 . Retrieval Number: A1293109119/2019©BEIESP DOI: 10.35940/ijeat.A1293.129219

18. Triangle Calculator - shows all steps - Math Portal https://www.mathportal.org/calculators/plane-geometry-calculators/sine-cosine-law-calculator.php

19. wolframalpha.com . sine law calculator

https://www.wolframalpha.com/input/?i=sine+law+calculator

20. Law of Sines Calculator - Symbolab https://www.symbolab.com/solver/law-of-sines-calculator

8. Education 4.0 Calculator Workshop at Phor Tay Secondary School.

9. Feedback from Phor Tay Secondary School teacher.

i) Teacher Low Mun Lai

Feedback For The Solution Of Triangle Seminar

Teacher's Name: _LOW MUN LAI_   School: _SMJK PHOR TAY_

Mobile Phone (Optional): _012-4479788_   Email (optional): _____

1. Before the seminar, do you know Peter Chew Rule, Method and Triangle Diagrams? Yes ☐ , No ☑

Description (optional): _____

2. Do you agree that Peter Chew's Method and Peter Chew's Rule are easier than the current method

to solve the same triangle problem?   Yes ☑ , No ☐

Description (optional): _____

3. Before the seminar, did you know how to solve all the triangle problems easily, just use one Rule

and only once?   Yes ☐ , No ☑

Description (optional): _____

4. After the seminar, do you know how to solve all the triangle problems easily, just use one Rule and

only once?   Yes ☑ , No ☐

Description (optional): _____

5. Do you agree that Peter Chew's Triangle Diagram makes teaching and learning Triangle Solution

Topic (KSSM, Level 4) easier and more effective?   Yes ☑ , No ☐

Description (optional): _____

6. Do you agree to introduce the Malaysian Ministry of Education to add Peter Chew's Triangle

Diagram to the Additional Mathematics book to make the teaching and learning of Solution of

Triangle Topics (KSSM, Level 4) more effective?   Yes ☑ , No ☐

Description (optional): _____

Thank you for your feedback!

Feedback Education 4.0 Calculator Workshop

Teacher's Name: _LOW MUN LAI_   School: _CMJK PHOR TAY_

Mobile Phone (Optional):_____   Email (optional): _____

1. Do you agree that Educational 4.0 Calculator is easy to use?   Yes ☑, No ☐

Description (optional): _____

2. After attending the Educational 4.0 Calculator Workshop, do you know how to use the Educational 4.0 Calculator to find the final answer to the triangle problem?   Yes ☑, No ☐

Description (optional): _____

3. After attending the Educational 4.0 Calculator Workshop, You know how to use the Educational 4.0 Calculator to solve all triangle problems Step by Step with one Rule and only once. Yes ☑, No ☐

Description (optional): _____

4. Educational 4.0 Calculator has Malaysian and English versions, which version do you prefer?

Malay Version ☐,   English Version ☑

Description (optional): _____

5. Do you agree that the Educational 4.0 Calculator learning method makes teaching and learning Solution of triangle Topics (KSSM, Level 4) more effective ?   Yes ☑, No ☐

Description (optional): _____

6. Do you agree to introduce the Malaysian Ministry of Education to add the Education 4.0 calculator learning method to the current learning method to make teaching and learning more effective?

Yes ☑, No ☐

Description (optional): _____

Thank you for your feedback!

ii) Teacher Khaw Heng Yeam

Feedback For The Solution Of Triangle Seminar

Teacher's Name: _Khaw Heng Yeam_   School: _SMJK PHOR TAY_

Mobile Phone (Optional): _016437010_   Email (optional): _khawhy@yahoo.com_

1. Before the seminar, do you know Peter Chew Rule, Method and Triangle Diagrams? Yes ☐, No ☑

Description (optional): _____

2. Do you agree that Peter Chew's Method and Peter Chew's Rule are easier than the current method to solve the same triangle problem?   Yes ☑, No ☐

Description (optional): _____

3. Before the seminar, did you know how to solve all the triangle problems easily, just use one Rule and only once?   Yes ☐, No ☑

Description (optional): _____

4. After the seminar, do you know how to solve all the triangle problems easily, just use one Rule and only once?   Yes ☑, No ☐

Description (optional): _____

5. Do you agree that Peter Chew's Triangle Diagram makes teaching and learning Triangle Solution Topic (KSSM, Level 4) easier and more effective?   Yes ☑, No ☐

Description (optional): _____

6. Do you agree to introduce the Malaysian Ministry of Education to add Peter Chew's Triangle Diagram to the Additional Mathematics book to make the teaching and learning of Solution of Triangle Topics (KSSM, Level 4) more effective?   Yes ☑, No ☐

Description (optional): _____

Thank you for your feedback!

Feedback Education 4.0 Calculator Workshop

Teacher's Name: _Khaw Heng Yeah_ School: _SMJK PHOR TAY_

Mobile Phone (Optional): _0164370180_ Email (optional): _Khawhy @ yahoo.com_

1. Do you agree that Educational 4.0 Calculator is easy to use?   Yes ☑, No ☐

Description (optional): _____

2. After attending the Educational 4.0 Calculator Workshop, do you know how to use the Educational 4.0 Calculator to find the final answer to the triangle problem?   Yes ☑, No ☐

Description (optional): _____

3. After attending the Educational 4.0 Calculator Workshop, You know how to use the Educational 4.0 Calculator to solve all triangle problems Step by Step with one Rule and only once. Yes ☑, No ☐

Description (optional): _____

4. Educational 4.0 Calculator has Malaysian and English versions, which version do you prefer?

Malay Version ☐,   English Version ☑

Description (optional): _____

5. Do you agree that the Educational 4.0 Calculator learning method makes teaching and learning Solution of triangle Topics (KSSM, Level 4) more effective ?   Yes ☑, No ☐

Description (optional): _____

6. Do you agree to introduce the Malaysian Ministry of Education to add the Education 4.0 calculator learning method to the current learning method to make teaching and learning more effective?

Yes ☑, No ☐

Description (optional): _____

Thank you for your feedback!

iii) Teacher Teoh Kheng Leong

Feedback For The Solution Of Triangle Seminar

Teacher's Name: Teoh Kheng Leong   School: SMJK Phor Tay

Mobile Phone (Optional): _____   Email (optional): _____

1. Before the seminar, do you know Peter Chew Rule, Method and Triangle Diagrams? Yes ☐, No ☑

Description (optional): _____

2. Do you agree that Peter Chew's Method and Peter Chew's Rule are easier than the current method to solve the same triangle problem?   Yes ☑, No ☐

Description (optional): _____

3. Before the seminar, did you know how to solve all the triangle problems easily, just use one Rule and only once?   Yes ☐, No ☑

Description (optional): _____

4. After the seminar, do you know how to solve all the triangle problems easily, just use one Rule and only once?   Yes ☑, No ☐

Description (optional): _____

5. Do you agree that Peter Chew's Triangle Diagram makes teaching and learning Triangle Solution Topic (KSSM, Level 4) easier and more effective?   Yes ☑, No ☐

Description (optional): _____

6. Do you agree to introduce the Malaysian Ministry of Education to add Peter Chew's Triangle Diagram to the Additional Mathematics book to make the teaching and learning of Solution of Triangle Topics (KSSM, Level 4) more effective?   Yes ☑, No ☐

Description (optional): _____

Thank you for your feedback!

Feedback Education 4.0 Calculator Workshop

Teacher's Name: _Teoh Kheng Leong_   School: _SMJK Phor Tay_
Mobile Phone (Optional): _012-5840398_   Email (optional): _tkl-simplybest @ hotmail.co_

1. Do you agree that Educational 4.0 Calculator is easy to use?   Yes ☑, No ☐
Description (optional): _____

2. After attending the Educational 4.0 Calculator Workshop, do you know how to use the Educational 4.0 Calculator to find the final answer to the triangle problem?   Yes ☑, No ☐
Description (optional): _____

3. After attending the Educational 4.0 Calculator Workshop, You know how to use the Educational 4.0 Calculator to solve all triangle problems Step by Step with one Rule and only once. Yes ☑, No ☐
Description (optional): _____

4. Educational 4.0 Calculator has Malaysian and English versions, which version do you prefer?
Malay Version ☐,   English Version ☑
Description (optional): _____

5. Do you agree that the Educational 4.0 Calculator learning method makes teaching and learning Solution of triangle Topics (KSSM, Level 4) more effective ? Yes ☑, No ☐
Description (optional): _____

6. Do you agree to introduce the Malaysian Ministry of Education to add the Education 4.0 calculator learning method to the current learning method to make teaching and learning more effective?
Yes ☑, No ☐
Description (optional): _____

Thank you for your feedback!

iv) Teacher Khong Wei Seng

Feedback For The Solution Of Triangle Seminar

Teacher's Name: _Khong Wei Seng_   School: _SMJK Phor Tay_

Mobile Phone (Optional): _017-493 2503_   Email (optional): _____

1. Before the seminar, do you know Peter Chew Rule, Method and Triangle Diagrams? Yes □, No ☑

Description (optional): _____

2. Do you agree that Peter Chew's Method and Peter Chew's Rule are easier than the current method to solve the same triangle problem?   Yes ☑, No □

Description (optional): _____

3. Before the seminar, did you know how to solve all the triangle problems easily, just use one Rule and only once?   Yes □, No ☑

Description (optional): _____

4. After the seminar, do you know how to solve all the triangle problems easily, just use one Rule and only once?   Yes ☑, No □

Description (optional): _____

5. Do you agree that Peter Chew's Triangle Diagram makes teaching and learning Triangle Solution Topic (KSSM, Level 4) easier and more effective?   Yes ☑, No □

Description (optional): _____

6. Do you agree to introduce the Malaysian Ministry of Education to add Peter Chew's Triangle Diagram to the Additional Mathematics book to make the teaching and learning of Solution of Triangle Topics (KSSM, Level 4) more effective?   Yes ☑, No □

Description (optional): _____

Thank you for your feedback!

Feedback Education 4.0 Calculator Workshop

Teacher's Name: _Khong We) Seng_ School: _SMJK phor Tay_

Mobile Phone (Optional): _017-493 2503_ Email (optional): _____

1. Do you agree that Educational 4.0 Calculator is easy to use? Yes ☑, No ☐

Description (optional): _____

2. After attending the Educational 4.0 Calculator Workshop, do you know how to use the Educational 4.0 Calculator to find the final answer to the triangle problem? Yes ☑, No ☐

Description (optional): _____

3. After attending the Educational 4.0 Calculator Workshop, You know how to use the Educational 4.0 Calculator to solve all triangle problems Step by Step with one Rule and only once. Yes ☑, No ☐

Description (optional): _____

4. Educational 4.0 Calculator has Malaysian and English versions, which version do you prefer?

Malay Version ☑, English Version ☑

Description (optional): _both_

5. Do you agree that the Educational 4.0 Calculator learning method makes teaching and learning Solution of triangle Topics (KSSM, Level 4) more effective ? Yes ☑, No ☐

Description (optional): _____

6. Do you agree to introduce the Malaysian Ministry of Education to add the Education 4.0 calculator learning method to the current learning method to make teaching and learning more effective?

Yes ☑, No ☐

Description (optional): _____

Thank you for your feedback!

v) Teacher Png Ying Hua

Feedback For The Solution Of Triangle Seminar

Teacher's Name: _Png Ying Hua_   School: _SMK PH OR ZHY_

Mobile Phone (Optional): _017415836 2_   Email (optional): _yvh~@hotmail.my_

1. Before the seminar, do you know Peter Chew Rule, Method and Triangle Diagrams? Yes ☑ , No ☐

Description (optional): _____

2. Do you agree that Peter Chew's Method and Peter Chew's Rule are easier than the current method to solve the same triangle problem?   Yes ☑ , No ☐

Description (optional): _____

3. Before the seminar, did you know how to solve all the triangle problems easily, just use one Rule and only once?   Yes ☑ , No ☐

Description (optional): _____

4. After the seminar, do you know how to solve all the triangle problems easily, just use one Rule and only once?   Yes ☑ , No ☐

Description (optional): _____

5. Do you agree that Peter Chew's Triangle Diagram makes teaching and learning Triangle Solution Topic (KSSM, Level 4) easier and more effective?   Yes ☑ , No ☐

Description (optional): _____

6. Do you agree to introduce the Malaysian Ministry of Education to add Peter Chew's Triangle Diagram to the Additional Mathematics book to make the teaching and learning of Solution of Triangle Topics (KSSM, Level 4) more effective?   Yes ☑ , No ☐

Description (optional): _____

Thank you for your feedback!

Feedback Education 4.0 Calculator Workshop

Teacher's Name: _Png Ying Hue_   School: _SMJK PHOR TAY_

Mobile Phone (Optional): _0174158362_   Email (optional): _ynhua @ hotmail.my_

1. Do you agree that Educational 4.0 Calculator is easy to use?   Yes ☑, No ☐

Description (optional): _____

2. After attending the Educational 4.0 Calculator Workshop, do you know how to use the Educational 4.0 Calculator to find the final answer to the triangle problem?   Yes ☑, No ☐

Description (optional): _____

3. After attending the Educational 4.0 Calculator Workshop, You know how to use the Educational 4.0 Calculator to solve all triangle problems Step by Step with one Rule and only once. Yes ☑, No ☐

Description (optional): _____

4. Educational 4.0 Calculator has Malaysian and English versions, which version do you prefer?

Malay Version ☐,   English Version ☑

Description (optional): _____

5. Do you agree that the Educational 4.0 Calculator learning method makes teaching and learning Solution of triangle Topics (KSSM, Level 4) more effective ?   Yes ☑, No ☐

Description (optional): _____

6. Do you agree to introduce the Malaysian Ministry of Education to add the Education 4.0 calculator learning method to the current learning method to make teaching and learning more effective?

Yes ☑, No ☐

Description (optional): _____

Thank you for your feedback!

vi) Teacher YKK

Feedback For The Solution Of Triangle Seminar

Teacher's Name: _____YKK_____   School: _____Su Yk Pluor Tay_____

Mobile Phone (Optional): _____   Email (optional): _____

1. Before the seminar, do you know Peter Chew Rule, Method and Triangle Diagrams? Yes ☐ , No ☑

Description (optional): _____

2. Do you agree that Peter Chew's Method and Peter Chew's Rule are easier than the current method to solve the same triangle problem?   (Yes ☑), No ☐

Description (optional): _____

3. Before the seminar, did you know how to solve all the triangle problems easily, just use one Rule and only once?   Yes ☐ , No ☑

Description (optional): _____

4. After the seminar, do you know how to solve all the triangle problems easily, just use one Rule and only once?   Yes ☑ , No ☐

Description (optional): _____

5. Do you agree that Peter Chew's Triangle Diagram makes teaching and learning Triangle Solution Topic (KSSM, Level 4) easier and more effective?   Yes ☑ , No ☐

Description (optional): _____

6. Do you agree to introduce the Malaysian Ministry of Education to add Peter Chew's Triangle Diagram to the Additional Mathematics book to make the teaching and learning of Solution of Triangle Topics (KSSM, Level 4) more effective?   Yes ☑ , No ☐

Description (optional): _____

Thank you for your feedback!

Feedback Education 4.0 Calculator Workshop

Teacher's Name: _____YKK_____   School: _____Sunfle Mhor Tay_____

Mobile Phone (Optional): _____   Email (optional): _____

1. Do you agree that Educational 4.0 Calculator is easy to use?   Yes ☑, No ☐

Description (optional): _____

2. After attending the Educational 4.0 Calculator Workshop, do you know how to use the Educational 4.0 Calculator to find the final answer to the triangle problem?   Yes ☑, No ☐

Description (optional): _____

3. After attending the Educational 4.0 Calculator Workshop, You know how to use the Educational 4.0 Calculator to solve all triangle problems Step by Step with one Rule and only once. Yes ☑, No ☐

Description (optional): _____

4. Educational 4.0 Calculator has Malaysian and English versions, which version do you prefer?

Malay Version ☐,   English Version ☑

Description (optional): _____

5. Do you agree that the Educational 4.0 Calculator learning method makes teaching and learning Solution of triangle Topics (KSSM, Level 4) more effective ? Yes ☑, No ☐

Description (optional): _____

6. Do you agree to introduce the Malaysian Ministry of Education to add the Education 4.0 calculator learning method to the current learning method to make teaching and learning more effective?

Yes ☑, No ☐

Description (optional): _____

Thank you for your feedback!

10. Feedback from the SISC+ Science and Mathematics Officer of the Seberang Prai Tengah District Education Office, Penang, Tuan Ong Khye Ching.

Aktiviti	Kursus Pemantapan Pedagogi Guru Matematik Tambahan Sekolah Menengah Dearah Seberang Prai Tengah Tahun 2022
Tarikh	1 Disember 2022 (Khamis)
Masa	8:30am – 12:30pm
Tempat	Bilik Mesyuarat Utama PPD SPT
Penceramah	Prof Peter Chew
Ulasan	Saya teruja dengan perkongsian Dr Peter Chew mengenai Petua , Kaedah dan Gambar Rajah Peter Chew bagi penyesaian segi tiga dan Kalkulator Pendidikan 4.0. Perkongsian ini menambah ilmu pengetahuan dan kemahiran baharu dalam pengajaran topik penyelesaian segi tiga. Penggunaan Petua, Kaedah dan Gambar Rajah Peter Chew dapat menyelesaikan masalah segitiga dengan penyelesaian yang mudah. Kalkulator Pendidikan 4.0 yang diperkenalkan oleh Dr Peter Chew merupakan aplikasi pdp baharu dapat membantu meningkatkan kualiti keberkesanan pembelajaran murid dalam topik penyelesaian segi tiga (KSSM Matematik Tamabahan Tingkatan 4). Saya berharap ilmu dan kemahiran yang baharu ini agar dapat disebarluas kepada guru-guru Matematik Tambahan di seluruh Malaysia. Saya bercadang bahawa Petua, Kaedah dan Gambar Rajah Peter Chew dapat diterbitkan dalam kurikulum Matematik Tambahan supaya menyediakan lebih alternatif pilihan kepada murid-murid dalam penyelesaian masalah segi tiga.

Disediakan oleh : Ong Khye Ching
Pegawai SISC+ Sains dan Matematik
Pejabat Pendidikan Daerah Seberang Prai Tengah,
Pulau Pinang

Tarikh : 2 Disember 2022

11. Feedback from Additional Mathematics Teacher SMJK Chio Min, Kulim, Kedah, Teacher Phong Bee Bee.

Education 4.0 Calculator Workshop Feedback

School : SMK CHIO MIN

Teacher Name: PHONG BEE BEE   Class: —

Add Math Average marks : —

Question:

1. Did you learn the sine rule and cosine rule before the workshop?

Yes ✓, No ☐

2. Do you think Education 4.0 Calculator, Peter Chew Triangle Diagram Calculator easy to use?

Yes ✓, No ☐

Description (optional): Easy to install and easy to access off line.

3. After attending the **Education 4.0 Calculator Workshop**, do you know how to use Education 4.0 Calculator, Peter Chew Triangle Diagram Calculator to find the final answer of triangle problem?

Yes ✓, No ☐

Description (optional) : user friendly.

4. After attending the **Education 4.0 Calculator Workshop**, You know how to use the Education 4.0 Calculator, Peter Chew Triangle Diagram Calculator to solve triangle problems Step by Step with a single rule, such as the sine or cosine rule?

Yes ✓, No ☐

Description (optional): the steps are clear and systematically

5. Original learning method or Education 4.0 calculator learning method, which one do you prefer?

Original learning method ☐ , Education 4.0 calculator learning method ✓

Description (optional) : more interesting,

6. Do you recommend Malaysia to use the Education 4.0 calculator learning method instead of the original learning method ?

Yes ✓, No ☐

Description (optional) : Easy to understand, very suitable for students and convenient to use.

Thanks for your feedback !

Milton Keynes UK
Ingram Content Group UK Ltd.
UKHW020924201123
432908UK00021B/3214